You've Got to be You Snoopy

Selected Cartoons From
You've Come A Long Way,
Charlie Brown, Volume 2

Charles M. Schulz

CORONET BOOKS
Hodder Fawcett, London

First published 1976 by
Fawcett Publications, Inc., New York

Coronet Edition 1977

Printed in Great Britain for Hodder
Fawcett Ltd., Mill Road, Dunton Green,
Sevenoaks, Kent (Editorial Office: 47
Bedford Square, London, WC1 3DP) by
C. Nicholls & Company Ltd.,
The Philips Park Press, Manchester

ISBN 0 340 21983 1

Columbus Day
by Sally Brown
THIS IS A REPORT FOR SCHOOL
I SEE
Columbus Day was a very brave man. He wanted to sail around the world.
"I can give you three ships, Mr. Day," said the Queen.
GOOD LUCK
THANK YOU
SCHULZ

Dear Little Red Haired Girl,
Evening is coming on.
I wish it were snowing huge white flakes, and you and I were walking along holding hands and.
A LOT OF GREAT LETTERS NEVER GET MAILED
SCHULZ

WOULDN'T IT BE SOMETHING IF I COULD BE WALKING ALONG IN THE SNOW WITH THAT LITTLE RED-HAIRED GIRL?
MAYBE SHE'D BE WEARING FURRY MITTENS, AND MAYBE WE'D CLIMB TO THE TOP OF THIS BIG HILL, AND SLIDE DOWN ON A TOBOGGAN, AND WHEN WE WERE SLIDING DOWN, MAYBE I'D PUT MY ARMS AROUND HER, AND...
WOW!
NO WAY!
SCHULZ

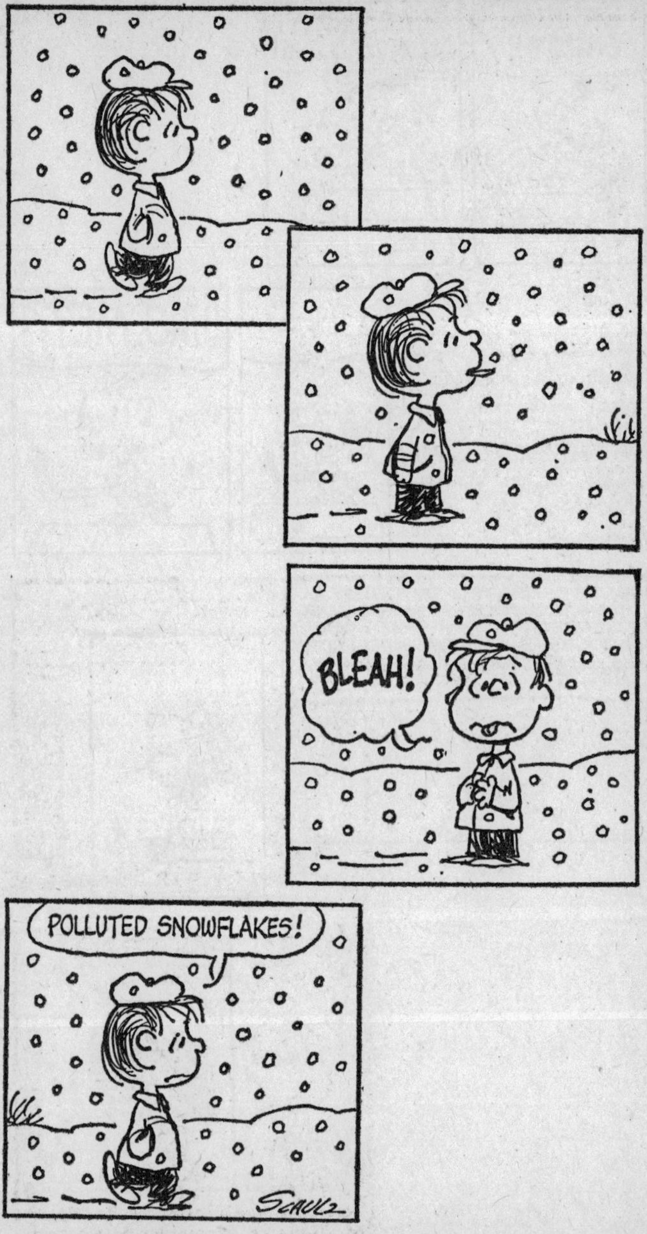
BLEAH!
POLLUTED SNOWFLAKES!
SCHULZ

FOR THE LOVE OF PEANUTS

All these books are available at your local bookshop or newsagent, or can be ordered direct from the publisher. Just tick the titles you want and fill in the form below.
Prices and availability subject to change without notice.

CORONET BOOKS, P.O. Box 11, Falmouth, Cornwall.
Please send cheque or postal order, and allow the following for postage and packing:
U.K. – One book 19p plus 9p per copy for each additional book ordered, up to a maximum of 73p.
B.F.P.O. and EIRE – 19p for the first book plus 9p per copy for the next 6 books, thereafter 3p per book.
OTHER OVERSEAS CUSTOMERS – 20p for the first book and 10p per copy for each additional book.

Name ....

Address ....

....